Faces of the Universe

by Tom Lumbrazo
and Carol Lumbrazo

Printed in China

Published by BAEB Publishing
BAEB Publishing
201 Sand Creek Road, Ste H
Brentwood, CA 94513
888-775-BAEB (2232)

To order go to www.whenangelstouch.com

When Angels Touch, LLC
1191 Douglas Blvd., #85-140
Roseville, CA 95661
916-782-8408

ISBN: 978-0-9795107-6-2

Dedicated to Our Parents

John and Fern Lumbrazo—Thank you for all of your support and trust in us. Your guidance and love makes this endeavor so meaningful.

Harold and Margaret McClure—Thank you for being loving and supportive. From King Arthur and Merlin to UFO's, you always gave me the freedom to BELIEVE! in things magical and unusual.

About the Authors

Tom Lumbrazo is an author, photographer, planner, artist, and nephologist. Tom has a background in government and has spent 40 years as a city planner and planning consultant in the Sacramento, California region.

Tom could be described as a practical, levelheaded person who worked hard all his life. Eight years ago, he had a near-death experience during a major car accident. Seconds before the accident, a strong male voice in his car directed him to slow from 60 mph to 35 mph. Tom listened to this voice immediately, and by going 35 mph, his life was saved. Since that incident, his life has changed dramatically, leading him into the fields of photography, art, and now author.

With this change in life interests, Tom has gained the ability to see images and messages in such places as clouds, rocks, sidewalks, and in the paranormal sense.

One of the things you might call Tom is a neo-nephologist. A nephologist is one who studies clouds. To Tom, a neo-nephologist might be one who studies clouds in a different way, a way that includes the patterns and messages coming from clouds.

Carol Lumbrazo spent her career working in libraries. Since childhood, books and reading have always been a significant part of her life. Travel was also one of her goals in life. The travels described in the stories and photos in this book have been like a dream come true for her.

Carol gains her support and guidance from Tom. His changes over the last few years and his new interests have given her a new perspective on life and many new interests to explore and follow.

How to Contact the Authors

Through their website: Whenangelstouch.com

Through email: Tom@whenangelstouch.com
Carol@whenangelstouch.com

Through phone: 916-768-9334

Through mail: When Angels Touch, LLC
1911 Douglas Blvd. #85-140
Roseville, California 95661

A Message from Carol and Tom

We have prepared this book to enlighten and share the images found in such unlikely places as the clouds, rocks, sidewalks, and in all that is around us. We hope your life is blessed with the desire to see the "unseen" and to speculate what all this may mean relative to our existence.

By discovering such images as presented in this book, we have found great feelings of Love, Joy, Wonder, and Generosity. Our world is the home to all of us. Its simplicity and complexity at the same time is magnificent, and amazing to contemplate. Hopefully, we are all wise enough to preserve this incredible place for future generations.

Paths of Destiny

For the Earth was Her domain and His was the Stars

Separately their paths were unfulfilled

Their Destiny-To find each other in this Time

To travel together

To explore the meaning of all Things

Together, there was Wonder and Excitement

Searching and Learning

Humbleness and Generosity

Love and Passion

And All was Revealed

By Tom and Carol Lumbrazo

Acknowledgments

THE GREAT SPIRIT

Some of our Native American ancestors have a term for God, THE GREAT SPIRIT. The one that creates all.

Without THE GREAT SPIRIT, this book would be much less meaningful. Most of us wonder what life is all about. Images from the sky, the earth, even the air around us, give all of us some insight into our existence. Perhaps the answers lie in creation that THE GREAT SPIRIT has provided to us.

There are cloud images on pages 64-65 which look to us like a Native American Chief or leader. Perhaps this is THE GREAT SPIRIT showing its presence for us to contemplate.

PSYCHIC FRIENDS

Many of our friends are blessed with incredible intuitive talents. We have found them to be gifted, wise, giving, and loving. Without their guidance and belief in us, this journey of discovery would be so much more difficult, maybe impossible. A special thank you goes to Linda, Francie Marie, Kathleen, Kimberly, Emerald, Beata, and Frederic.

Table of Contents

Chapters

Forward

This Forward is very special to us. Many of our intuitive friends have offered their perspectives to share with you.   – Tom and Carol

From Frederic Delarue:

Thank you Tom and Carol for your humble act to bring awareness, through your books, to what Nature offers all of us very generously. It is eye-opening to all.

Often we think answers are out of reach and are only reserved to psychics. However, the reason why "psychics" can see clearly for you, is because they are not attached to the impact of the answer, therefore, they are not limited to any direct emotions. So we think or we have learned to think that answers are complicated to get.

Who said that most answers lay in plain sight, that's why we don't see them? We all can be our own psychic and medium, when we learn to see, and listen to the signs that Nature delivers so generously. A good way to do so is when you find yourself preoccupied by a worry, a decision to make or a situation that seems difficult, start watching the clouds forming, or watch a rock formation and start seeing beyond the rock, and see the signs which can be faces formed naturally or etched into a rock formation, and anywhere else.

Be open enough because signs can be everywhere. You can be wondering at something, looking down to your carpet and seeing beyond the carpet and start seeing faces or a sign that will give you a feeling that this is YOUR answer.

Tom's books are the beginning for you to see life from a different perspective.

Frederic Delarue
Music Composer and Author of "Eyes of Your Heart"
www.FredericDelarue.com

From Linda Schooler:

I first met Tom a few years ago when he came to me for a psychic reading. I've been an intuitive consultant for over 20 years and initially considered this to be just another reading. In fact it was to be much more than that, and as I soon learned, Tom would become a friend and a teacher. During that first session in 2006, I relayed my impressions about what was coming up for him.

My first impression was that he would travel first to the U.S. Southwest and then extensive travel worldwide. Tom said that was not possible and that he did not have any interest nor the time for such travel. Within six months, he, for various reasons, started traveling in the Southwest to Los Angeles, Palm Springs, New Mexico, and Arizona. And then the travel started in 2007 to Peru, then England and France, Hawaii, and Egypt.

Little did he know that the reason for such travel was to connect him with the planet, and to take pictures of the clouds, which have led to this book.

My next impression for him was that after he came back from Peru, that he would begin painting immediately. Tom's reaction was that this simply would not happen since he had absolutely no interest in painting and had no training or abilities in this area. To my amazement as well as Tom's, he began to paint within two weeks of coming back from Peru. Now his paintings are gaining much interest.

With his trips to Peru, England, France, Hawaii, and Egypt, his many paintings and photographs would capture the imagination. To have come so far in such a short time in his personal awakening required courage and trust. I am so impressed with his commitment to follow the clues that come to him in visions and messages on a daily basis. A new career was born as he followed through on this inner guidance. A fantastic voyage indeed was begun and continues.

In subsequent conversations since meeting Tom, I've had the pleasure of observing a most wondrous transformation. I now see a man truly connected to his inner truth who, by example, has facilitated similar transformations in others that he has encountered, encouraging them to pursue their own heartfelt journeys.

All of this transformation has led to his first book, "Journey to the Clouds--- Messages from the Sky" and this book, "Faces of the Universe". These books have brought attention for many about our sky and the many messages therein. Who has not gazed up at the clouds and pondered the infinite possibilities of creation? With his heart open and eye towards the sky, Tom has captured images that reveal to the mind's eye the ever-expanding horizons of imagination. After seeing Tom's photos, you will never look at the sky the same way. That's the truth.

It's been quite an honor to personally know Tom and be part of his incredible journey. I am excited about the newfound possibilities that life offers, and I continue to be transformed by being more open and aware. I thank Tom for that.

Linda Schooler
Psychic
(916) 725-9463
readings@lindaschooler.com
www.lindaschooler.com

From Francie Marie:

The day I met Tom Lumbrazo was the day I knew I had met someone special. A man on a separate journey than most here on Earth. A person who was transforming from a businessman to a man of insight, knowingness and ability. On that September day and the days that followed, I watched him grow and change in many ways. His spiritual strength began to grow through his travels, interactions with others, and the giving of himself and gifts he offered others. His transformation took many different turns as he began to paint, write, connect to the highest realm and open his heart to the healing of others. I have observed first hand this powerful transition that has taken place. I know God, a Higher Power, or Great Creator lives within Tom.

As I am a person with intuitive abilities and spiritual gifts, our meeting one another was truly an opportunity for both of us to grow and move forward. I have provided Tom with guidance and insight when answers were sought, yet our friendship has been based on a mutual exchange. I give insight and foresight and he walks the journey. He sees in others and in all things their inner essence, meaning and beauty. This book reveals his gifts. See what many can't see. The inner connection of each and every object. The energy of life force.

Francie Marie
intuitive, spiritual teacher and Angel reader
angelitevoices@cs.com
(530) 613-3679

From Kimberly:

The Equation of Creation: Within every human is the potential for unforeseen abilities and wisdom that surpasses anything that words can describe. There is an eternal beauty that is one with all of us—we are it, it is us. There is no distinction beyond what the mind can conceive. When we see ourselves from the vastness of what is, we know there is nothing we can do or say that separates us from this beauty.

Welcome to who you are, beyond your current name and form. Welcome to the wonder and beauty that is you—that is me—that we all are.

Kimberly
peacefulguidance.com

❖ ❖ ❖

From Emerald Alurin Stara:

When I first met Tom and his soul mate, Carol, Tom was burgeoning with the excitement and enthusiasm of an intrepid explorer. He was following a vision, a specific one, which led them to my Reading Sanctuary, and a greater one, calling him onto his Spiritual Path. The moment we met and I took out my Tarot Cards, he said "you won't believe this, but we were supposed to meet today." Tom then explained that he had a vision the night before...a vision represented by the adjacent drawing with the message to him to go to Nevada City and Grass Valley, California,

 which is where I work. Tom went on to explain he had not come to my town for at least the last 10 years. For some amazing reason, the vision he saw was an incredible representation of my Tarot Cards. At that moment, we both knew that we were supposed to meet for some grand reason.

The first session has led to a long-lasting friendship. Over the next several years, we would have many amazing sessions together. The Reading Sessions were always stunning with helpful information and insights, especially before and after Tom and Carol's many pilgrimage journeys to sacred sites around the world. The strong feeling of connecting for a purpose grew with each meeting and the mutual awareness that a support group, myself and others, was forming.

Tom's metamorphosis has been extraordinary, as his clarity and sense of purpose deepened and his vision continued to expand. The results—and they continue to evolve—are Tom's creative expressions as photographer, artist, poet, and communicator. I think you will agree that Tom has captured some amazing photographs in "Faces of the Universe" which help us understand the world around us in a different way. He is showing us that there is much more to our clouds than anyone ever believed. We thank you, Tom.

About Emerald Alurin Stara: Emerald is an Intuitive Consultant based in Northern California. She is also a Certified Crystal Awareness Instructor and the published author/illustrator of the fantasy tale *Princess Crystallina and the Star Children*. You may contact her by email at emstara@yahoo.com or by phone at (530) 274-3398.

Gifted from childhood with clairvoyant and clairsentient abilities, Emerald has lived and traveled throughout India, Hawaii, and mainland United States learning from Masters, Teachers, Healers, and her own in-depth growth work, study, and research. Emerald offers Oracle Tarot Card Readings to her clients, a spirit-based method of inquiry for wisdom, insight and understanding. Her unique interactive style combines extensive knowledge, including Numerology, with personal attunement for an experience that is comprehensive, enjoyable, and empowering.

Princess Crystallina and the Star Children follows the adventures of a magical galactic princess and her three young friends, Erin, Niki, and Michael, on a worldwide quest to benefit humanity. The reader or listener is transported with them to realms of angels, dolphins, wizards, pyramids, crystal chambers, Teachers of Light and ancient hidden repositories of knowledge and treasure. Discover the fantastic heritage that is revealed for the Star Children and the Earth. It is a tale that is uplifting and enjoyable for children and adults of all ages.

From Kathleen Scott:

I met Tom and Carol just about 3 years ago and in that short span of time, my life has changed. Last year, I had the chance to travel with them to New York City and then Egypt. Little did I know that this fortuitous meeting was much more than I could have dreamed.

In New York City, there was something going on with the clouds. There were no clouds, and then they would just appear like magic everywhere we went. One of the best times in NYC was seeing this incredible giant crystal at the American Express building at the 9/11 site. This crystal was a memorial to the 11 people that died that day from the American Express company. You must go and experience this memorial.

If you know Tom, you know how very caring and giving this man is...he always carries small crystals to give to everyone he meets to give them luck and healing. I have never known anyone like him and his beautiful wife who keeps him going.

Then off to Egypt. We went to Cairo, the Giza Plateau and the Great Pyramid, the Cairo Museum, to the Egypt-Sudan border with the Nefertiti Temple, Luxor, and so many more sacred places.

When at the Nefertiti Temple, a very special thing occurred. We all were given the large golden Ankh Key to the Temple...to hold it and absorb it. The security guards to the entry to the temple told us, "This is the Key" and gave it to us to hold together over Tom's left shoulder. What was so amazing is that our psychic friend Rebecca back in California predicted that Tom would be presented with a Key in Egypt over his left shoulder and that it would be very important. We were so amazed and in awe that it actually happened the way she predicted.

When we all went to the Pelea the Isis Temple, the energy was so amazing to me as I was given the message verbally, "I am Isis." All three of us were tuned into this energy in one of the healing rooms.

At the Temple of Karnack in Luxor, I was again stunned at the events. I was taking pictures of Tom and his crystals and when I looked at them later, there were many orbs around him as well as a large violet light surrounding him.

Last, we had our session in the Great Pyramid in the Cairo area. We went into the Queens and Kings Chambers. In the Kings Chamber, we had 2 hours of drumming and meditation. There were some negative energies at this time inside this chamber coming from some members of our larger tour group with which we travelled. During the session, I took the role of protector from these energies and channeled Isis who protected the three of us. And again another psychic prediction came true for Tom. He was told before the trip that he and Carol would become invisible inside the Great Pyramid. They did. During this rigorous and demanding drumming session, Tom went to the ground behind the sarcophagus and held Carol to comfort her against the strong energies there. By doing this, both of them were shielded by the sarcophagus and thus became invisible to all of the larger tour group.

A year later, the energies from our trip are still with us. We have all changed as a result. I believe Tom was especially activated and will continue to listen and follow his path. This book, "Faces of the Universe," is definitely a result of this trip, and these amazing energies we all experienced.

Kathleen Scott
CMT
Specializing in raindrop therapies,
sound and crystal healing,
reiki, and intuitive readings.
(916) 770-0118

From Beata Owens:

The first reading I have done for Tom was truly inspirational. Often, people come to me for a healing, clearing. Tom asked for communication. A beautiful vision came forth. Tom, an aspect of Archangel Michael, incarnating and now activated with others who are aspects of Archangels, helping to anchor pillars of light around the Earth. Two others in Spirit holding the North and South Poles. As each of these individual's travel coming closer together, the pillars interact and form new anchors between them. It is a beautiful geometric dance, guided by the hand of God in the ascension of Gaia. These special souls are part of the orchestra of God in this amazing awakening.

Since, I have watched Tom awaken in Spirit and in his abilities, and travel to various places as he is guided. He is sharing his visions and awakening others through his paintings, through the images in the clouds, showing us that Spirit, Angels, God are all around and within, inviting each of us to awaken within. Meet Tom and see the love and light of God shining through his eyes.

Revs. Geoffrey and Beata Owens are spiritual counselors, readers and healers. They founded the Sacred Heart Wellness Center in Auburn California, where they teach awareness and spiritual tools in order to empower people to awaken to their Spirit and heal themselves. For more information you can contact them at www.sacredheartwellnesscenter.com.

Introduction

Our first book of discovery was published in 2009. It is called *Journey to the Clouds, Messages from the Sky*. It was inspired by images we saw so clearly in cloud formations around the planet. Images of clouds in the form of angels, animals, parents, children, mythical creatures, and even aliens were presented.

Faces of the Universe goes beyond the clouds. It delves more precisely into the images imbeded in clouds, in rocks, in concrete sidewalks, and in the air around us. It challenges the reader to think about these images. What is being presented? Who created the images? Why? Are these messages to us? How are the images created? Are there other forms of life on the planet that we don't see?

Most of us are so busy in our daily lives that we miss this opportunity to explore such images around us. Some of us don't even want to think that such images could exist. Some of us are scared of these images. But clearly, they do exist. "Faces of the Universe" provides proof of their existence. This is why "Faces of the Universe" was written.

We hope that you will enjoy this book. Presented for you, we believe, are such things as clouds in the form of faces of human beings, animals, aliens, Native American images, cats, insects and more. Other cloud images, we believe, show angels, a king, a grandma, an elephant, and many others that defy explanation. Other cloud formations seem to indicate an event such as a mosquito insect with a man, or the appearance of a "mythical" god like Poseidon. And then there is the appearance of the Merkaba.

This book also includes images inside rocks and sidewalks....of creatures that we can recognize and those that we have never seen before.

Lastly, there are what might be called "paranormal" photographs with images of portals, minihunnas, orbs, alien entities, and flying saucers.

There is a lot to think about and absorb in *Faces of the Universe*. It is written to challenge the mind. It is about thinking about the world around us and wondering what we are missing, what we are not seeing and why this is all happening. Perhaps this book will help you to see such images and to study them at your own pace. Perhaps you will begin to look up into the sky to see the clouds, hoping to see something special, or to look down to the ground and wonder why there appears to be something unusual in that sidewalk or in a rock or rock formation.

For us, everyday brings another image to figure out, and to enjoy. It makes us feel a sense of togetherness with all of creation—the sky, ground, and the air. All three work together in harmony to allow us to exist. And what do we do with all these images, all this information? Each of us must deal with it. We may choose to ignore what we have seen. We may be too scared to think about it. We may just accept it. Or we may want to continue to explore it further...to satisfy our curiosity...to find out more...to find the ultimate answers.

Interpreting the Photographs

The authors have selected these photographs from thousands that they have taken in 2008 and 2009. Except for a few, the majority of these photographs were taken in the Northern California region. Where there is a different location than Northern California, the location will be cited for that photograph.

Where possible, each photograph will have some description or interpretation provided by the authors to help the reader understand what is being presented. As in the title of this book, many images in the photographs seem to have a face. Some faces appear human-like, and others are like animals, or even alien creatures. But faces, nonetheless. In order to see the images best, we suggest that you look at them close up, and also from a distance. This will add perspective and help your eyes adjust properly.

The authors believe that there is some intelligence guiding these images in the clouds. Surely, all of these images in these photographs could not be mere coincidence. So this raises questions like how is this done, why are they being presented to us in this manner, and what is being communicated.

Similarly, there are chapters in this book related to images in rocks and sidewalks, and photographs showing paranormal entities. From our perspective, the point of all this is that we are not alone in our world. There appear to be entities that we cannot see, but can communicate with us through clouds, rocks, sidewalks, and many other means. We just have to be aware and look.

Presentation of the Photographs

The presentation of the photographs in this book is done so that the reader can best see the images that have been found. There has been no manipulation or fabrication of any of the images in the photographs. Some photographs have been enhanced through color contrast so that the images could be better understood.

Nearly all of the photographs were taken with a Nikon D90 camera. Some were taken with an Apple iPhone.

Clouds over Northern California

CHAPTER I

How Most People See Clouds

Most people accept the clouds as a part of their daily lives. They are just there as billowy and formless. There are many types of clouds from cumulus, cirrus, and nimbus and more.

The three clouds presented here are just how most of us see clouds. They are just there with their individual beauty. But as you will see in the next chapters, there is much more to some clouds if you really look closely and remain open to the images that appear to you.

Clouds over the Grand Canyon, Arizona

Clouds over
Avebury, England

There appears to be three beings in the center of the photograph, all standing up and pointed in the right direction. They don't look human, but are clearly intelligent. What are they looking at or waiting for?

CHAPTER 2

Strange But True

This chapter presents clouds that just seem to be very strange. Some show very weird-looking creatures and their messages are perhaps unclear. What are they trying to tell us?

STRANGE BUT TRUE

The creature in the center appears to be animal-like, perhaps more like a bird of some sort. What do you think?

Popping out of this mass of clouds is a face or head in the center of the photograph. It has a head pointed to the left, with an eye, long snout, and open mouth. It looks more like an animal. Which animal do you think it is?

This elongated creature is shown in the right-center of the photograph, in a flying motion upwards. It has a head, long body, little arms, and perhaps wings. What could this be?

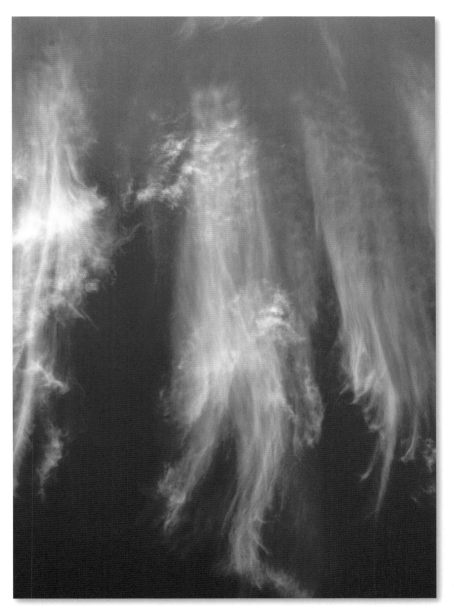

In the center is a big being of some sort. It looks like it has arms, a small head, and long body with legs and big feet. It looks like he is walking. Where is he going?

This is just a surreal photograph. The cloud seems to be forming into something. If you look in the center area of it, it appears to have the beginnings of a face—with two eyes and a smile. It is just beautiful.

All we can say is, Love is in the air.

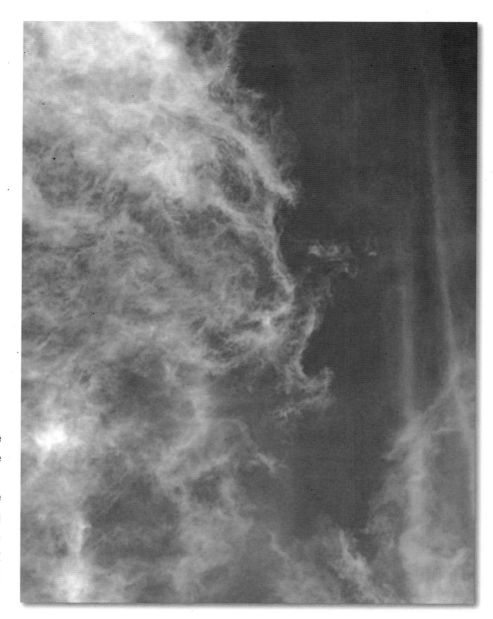

Look to the center of the photograph. There is a face of a being looking down to the right. It is more in an outline form.

This looks like a creature in the center-right. It appears to be lying backwards thereby showing us his belly, with his feet sticking out. Perhaps it is relaxing.

An insect type creature
standing up is shown.
Even it has little legs, a
head, and two antennae.
What is it telling us?

This human-type figure is floating in the sky. He looks very strong or muscular, with a head, a stocky body, and two legs.

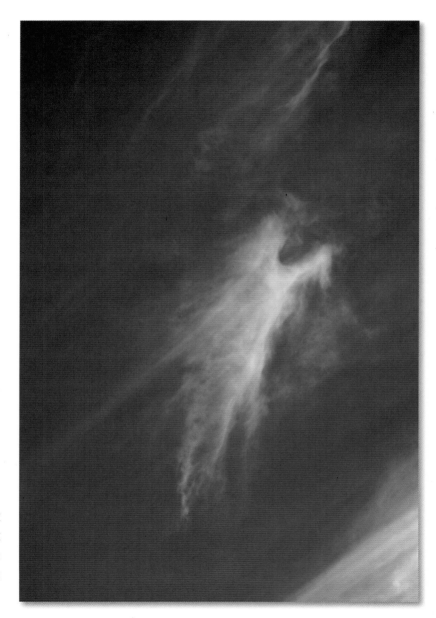

Another being that is flying to the right and upwards, with an arm out and an indication of wings.

What a mixture here! Perhaps there are three beings with faces—the lower one more shaped like a fish.

An animal-type creature posing like a cat or rabbit, perhaps in a sitting position. Its mouth is open and head is pointed to the right.

Although more difficult to see, this being is sitting, like in a chair, with its body facing to the left. You can make out its head, body and feet. This creature appears royal or powerful... perhaps it is Zeus, the mythical God.

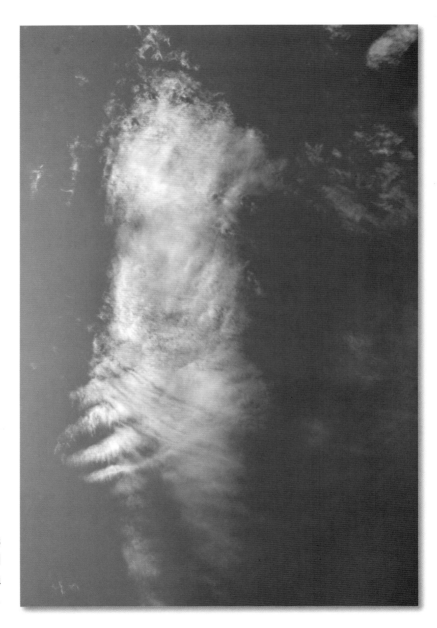

This creature is facing to the left and seems to have a large, claw-like hand.

This creature is
reaching for the sky.

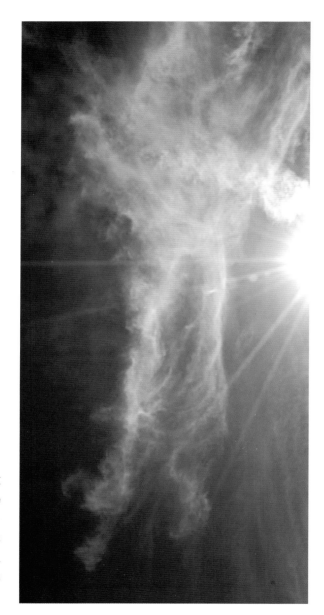

This one is almost ghostly. Taken near the sun, it shows a human-type body with legs and arms out, with a head and face. He is looking right at us.

Another animal-type figure floating in the sky, with its head pointed to the right. It has four legs, a body, and head with mouth and eyes. It is so interesting that there are no clouds around it...it just exists there floating.

This one is really interesting. In the center is a human type body from the waist upwards, showing arms, torso, and head area, but the face is hard to see. But look to the lower right—there is a dog, with its face looking back to the larger being. The dog seems to have a collar in the deeper white color.

Look at this creature,
with human-type form.
It is in the center, like it
is walking to the right.
It has a head, face,
eyes, and mouth open.

This looks like part of a creature—from the waist down, including the legs and feet.

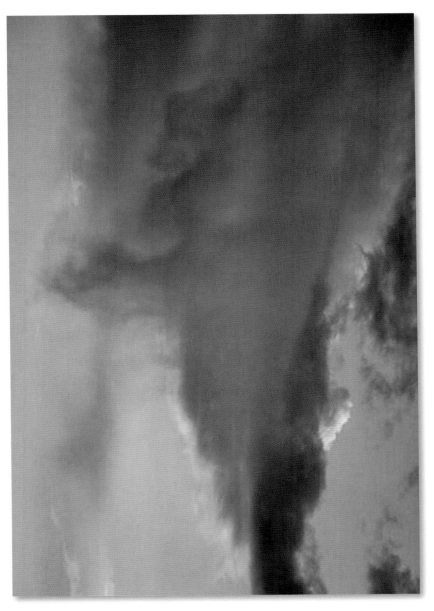

This one was taken at the Grand Canyon, Arizona. It shows a being standing up and pointing in the left direction, with arms outward, and head pointed left as well.

Taken at sunset, this being is either running or skating towards the left. It has a discernable head and face, large body, left arm out, and legs extended. How could all this be a coincidence? And where is it off to?

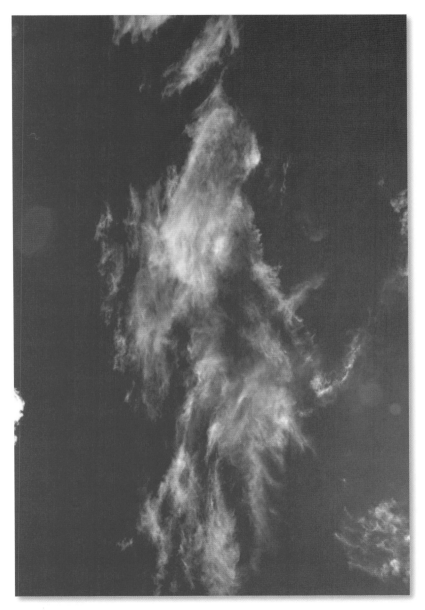

This is simply an incredible cloud. It is a female form, with its head pointed to the right, with her back to us. What is amazing is the appearance of long hair. She appears to be wearing a long flowing dress. Her face appears not to be human. What does she represent—a goddess, or a being from another realm?

This photograph shows the being in flight, with its wings, body and pointed head.

CHAPTER 3

Big Birds

This is the beginning of a series of small chapters that perhaps show something special in the clouds. These clouds may show an event happening, or may be so precise that there is no doubt that the clouds are speaking to all of us.

In this chapter, it is about a flying being—maybe a pterodactyl, as we understand their form to be—attacking another cloud being.

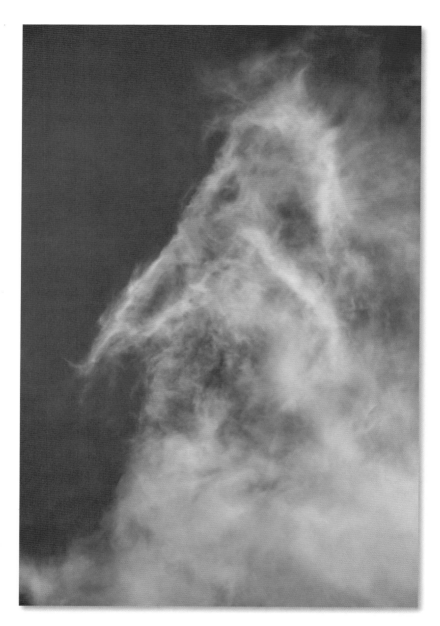

In this one, there is no doubt that this is a head, with a big eye, long beak structure pointing to the left.

The attack begins. The flying being is above the other cloud being below it, which is unaware of what is to happen. It is ready to attack, swooping down on the other being from above. This is an example of more than a cloud formed as a specific thing or being—it represents an event that is to happen.

The King and I Meet

The pictures and story in this chapter are amazing to us. These photographs were taken in July 2009 over our home. On this day, our publisher Patrick Shabram came from the San Francisco Bay area to our home in the Sacramento Valley in conjunction with the delivery of our first book—*Journey to the Clouds: Messages from the Sky.*

This cloud formed in the sky above us as we visited outside our home. Little did we really know what it was as we took the pictures, but we did know it was forming something.

We emailed these photographs to our psychic friend Francie Marie and she said that it was King Daniel. The image does appear to be very royal, with a man's face pointing downward, with perhaps a hand and arm upward with something in the hand. The head appears to have some sort of headdress. The face is very clear, with an eye, nose, mouth and chin.

If it was King Daniel being shown to us, then it is simply amazing. Our research indicates that King Daniel or Daniel was considered a dream interpreter, a saint and prophet approximately 600 BC in Babylon.

Why did this image appear for us? Who is it? What is the message that he was bringing to us? Did it have anything to do with our publisher and the delivery of our first book?

THE KING AND I MEET

THE KING AND I MEET

CHAPTER 5

Grandma is Always With Us

This series of three photographs appears to be a grandmother, perhaps as she was depicted in another time long ago. We get this impression from such things as the long torso with perhaps a long dress and head with the hair styled up. Her arms are closely held against her stomach, as if she is making some cookies in a bowl.

We get a warm feeling from these images. Perhaps you have had a grandmother like this one.

GRANDMA IS ALWAYS WITH US

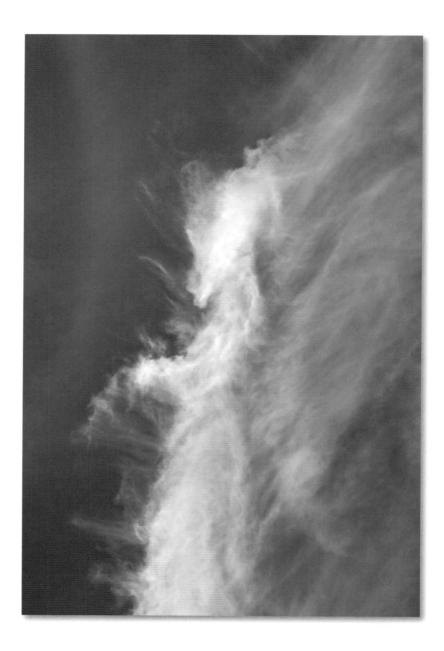

GRANDMA IS ALWAYS WITH US

CHAPTER 6

The Mosquito and the Man—The Hunt

This series of three photographs appears to portray an event. Perhaps the event is about the hunt.

We see a huge insect, the size of a human being or bigger. This insect looks like a giant mosquito, with its insect-type face, large eye, and large nose or stinger.

Below the giant mosquito is a man lying on his back, with his head shown at the lower left, the large chest, followed by his legs. The mosquito is looking down at him, poised to strike.

Could this be the depiction of the hunt by the mosquito of the man? The man is now captured and ready to be devoured.

After seeing these images, you can see that the clouds can be very precise in their form, and perhaps their messages.

THE MOSQUITO AND THE MAN–THE HUNT

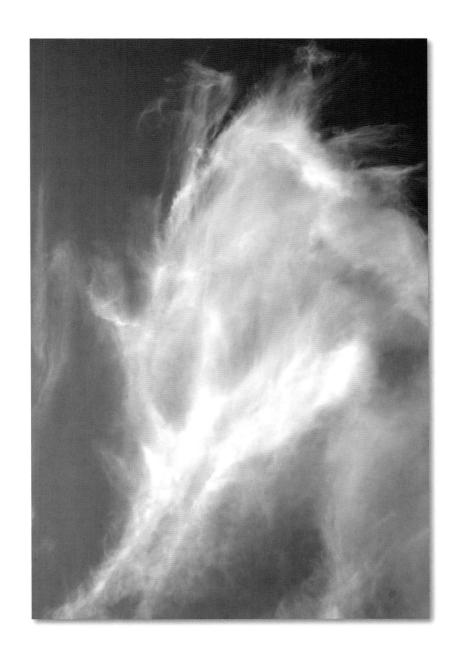

THE MOSQUITO AND THE MAN-THE HUNT

CHAPTER 7

The Great Spirit in the Sky

These three photographs give us the feeling of the Great Spirit. Many of the Native American cultures mention the Great Spirit, their term for God, or The Creator.

We see the human-type face in these clouds looking left. There are the indications of an eye, nose, mouth, but there are also indications of a headdress of some kind.

The appearance of this figure in the clouds makes one wonder why this is being shown to us. It is certainly a privilege to get to be a part of viewing this cloud. Could it represent The Great Spirit watching over all of us?

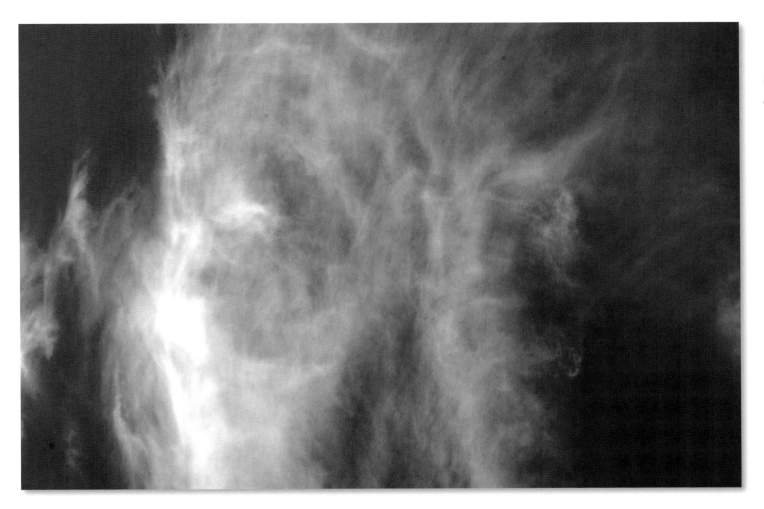

CHAPTER 8

The Adventures of Poseidon

These three photographs were taken in September 2009 at the Placer Art and Wine Festival, where up to 1,000 people attended. Near sunset, we noticed a little dot of a grayish cloud to the east. To the naked eye, one would normally dismiss it. But we sensed that there was something we should observe. We took several pictures, from normal to close up settings. Little did we know that we captured something special.

At first, the little cloud looked like it had some sort of form. Closer up, one can see a large head, with two eyes, perhaps a mustache or beard, and arms and legs. We think it is Poseidon, the mythical Greek God—the God of the Sea and Earthquakes. Images of Poseidon in literature and art appear much like this cloud. (You can compare these images with images of Poseidon in art by searching the Internet.) Nonetheless, this cloud is special. It was such a little cloud, but we are happy we captured the images in our camera. If this is a representation of Poseidon, what is being told to all of us? Perhaps the lesson is that there is something more to the "mythical gods" than we suspect.

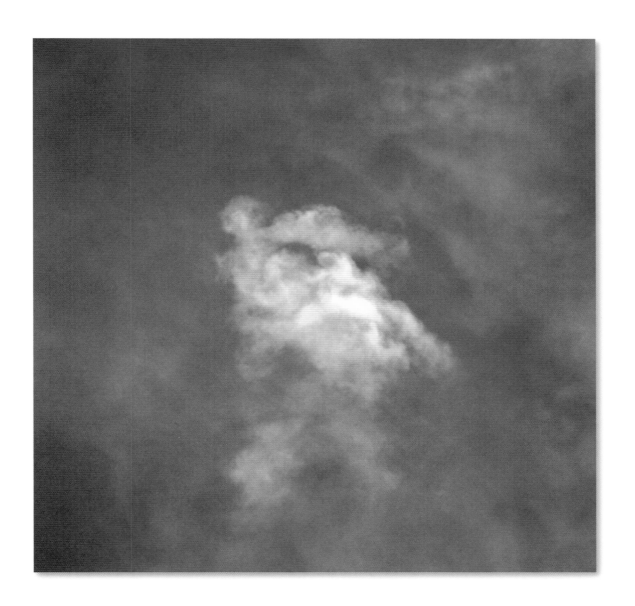

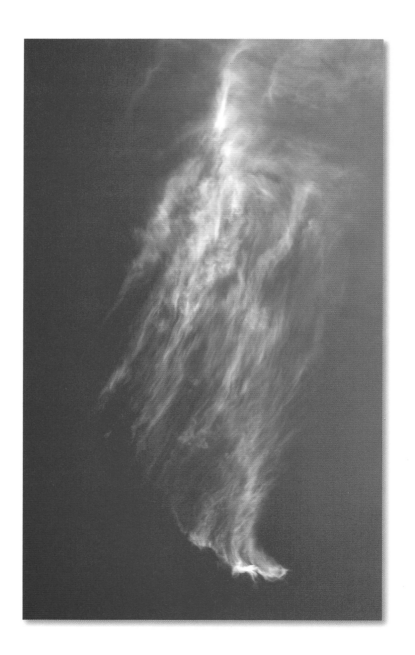

CHAPTER 9

Hanging Out

These three photographs have to make you wonder about the clouds. The first one indicates a human-type figure facing to the right with a body with arms, legs, feet, and torso. Perhaps it also shows flowing long hair or clothing.

The second one shows this being trying to reach or grab onto another creature. If you look closely, there is a small face in the bigger creature just behind the long appendages pointing to the left. Are these appendages arms of the bigger creature, and are both beings trying to reach each other?

The third photograph shows a closer up image of the being from the waist down. Clearly you can see the image of the legs and feet.

What is being shown here? What is the message?

HANGING OUT

CHAPTER 10

Out for a Ride

This series of five photographs depicts an event, which appears to be some sort of a being riding on another creature (similar to humans riding a horse).

In the first three photographs, you can see this elongated creature with a head to the far left. This head looks insect-like and its body gets bigger as you look to the right. Close-ups are provided of the head and you can see these appendages that come out from the head, giving the feeling of an insect creature. Farther to the right in a brighter white color is the being that is riding the creature. By its face, you can see the being is having a lot of fun as he is smiling.

The last two photographs appear to show a being sitting in a capsule as if enjoying the ride.

CHAPTER II

It Happened One Dark Night

These three photographs were taken at the Placer Wine and Art Fair in September 2009 at sunset. As sunset was approaching to the west, the clouds formed near the horizon in such a way that it caught our interest.

What formed was a huge image of a face in the sky. The image shows the face directly looking at us with a large mouth, eyes, and nose.

What was the importance of this image? Why was it shown? Who is it?

Many of the cloud images we capture offer insights as to what they might be. Some only make us think about why we see these images and some give us only small clues as to why they might be significant. What is important is that they make us open our minds to the possibilities and significance of life on our planet.

CHAPTER 12

Please Come to Me

This series of three photographs shows what appears to be an alien type of life form imbedded in a much larger cloud mass.

In the first one, you can see the larger cloud mass with a brighter cloud feature, which is the being. This photograph shows the context of the being within the cloud mass.

The next two show close-ups of the being. They show part of his body, and his arms extended to the left, with a large head and large eyes.

These images appear to indicate that he is asking us to embrace him, as he has his arms reaching out to us.

Would you go to him?

PLEASE COME TO ME

PLEASE COME TO ME

Water vapor cloud
formed by lava hitting
the ocean on the
Big Island of Hawaii.

CHAPTER 13

Faces of the Universe

This chapter exposes to us the many faces that can be seen in the clouds. From human, animal, alien, insect and many more, there are so many varieties of faces.

What comes to mind in a face—eyes, mouth, nose, head and head shape or form, and even expression. When you look at the variety of faces that are presented here, keep these factors in mind. You may not agree with us about the type or category of face shown, but you might agree that it is a face of some sort.

So why are faces being shown in the clouds? Why in these different forms or types? How can one explain so many faces in the clouds? Are they mimicking the types of life on our planet? Are they giving messages to us to consider?

Faces of the Human Kind

This section shows us faces that are uniquely human in form and expression. Comments from the authors are provided for some of these faces to give our impression of what it might be—you may or may not agree.

This incredible face is looking to the right. Some people that have seen it say it is Michael Jackson's face. Ironically, it was taken in mid June 2009 just weeks before his death. Whose face do you think it is?

This face shape
reminds us of
the moon...
"Man in the Moon."

Statesman or
elderly man.

May need a nose job!

This photograph has two faces... One is looking to the right and he looks like a wise guy type of character. The other face is looking directly at you.

This face is looking to the left. Is he extending his hand to us?

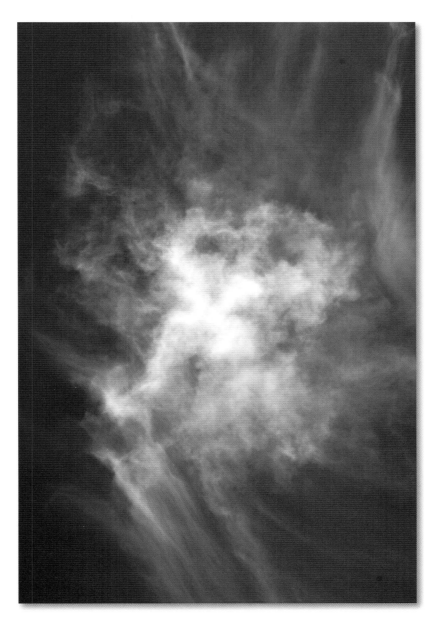

Baby face?

FACES OF THE UNIVERSE

If you look at this one from a distance, you might see the face of George Washington.

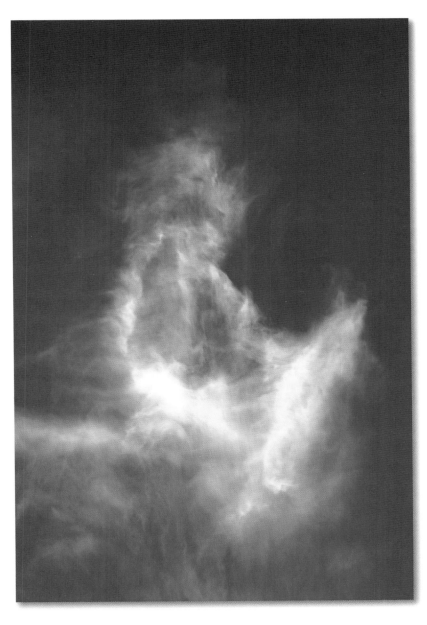

Is this a happy boy
sitting and playing?

FACES OF THE UNIVERSE

This one is looking
left. Does he seem
lost or is he sad?

FACES OF THE UNIVERSE

This one
is looking
down and
to the right.
He looks
powerful and
determined.

FACES OF THE UNIVERSE

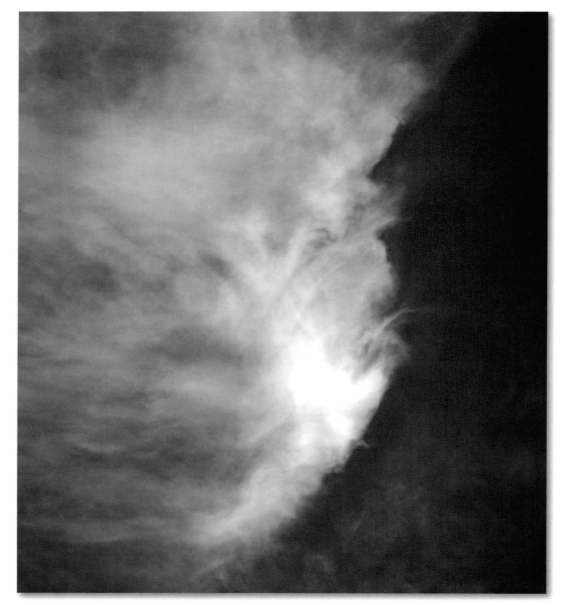

This face
is looking
upward to
the right.
The eyes
are very
defined. His
face is one
of anguish.

This face is a profile looking left. He looks like a mature man with confidence.

FACES OF THE UNIVERSE

I am searching but I
cannot see you!

Don't you think my
lips are beautiful?

Looking downward to the left is a face of happiness, joy, and friendship.

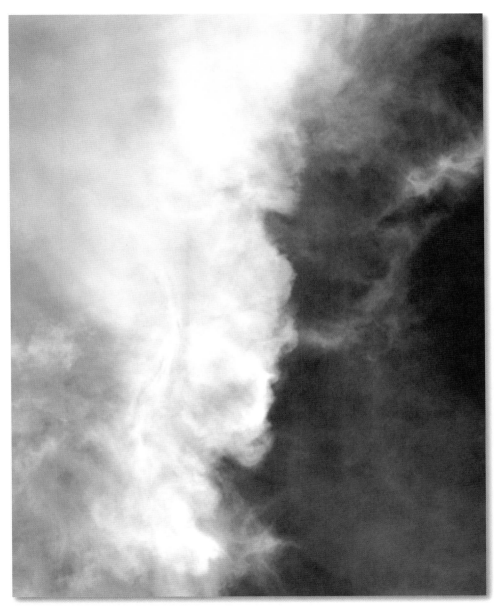

Looking away
to the right, this
face is confident
and powerful.

FACES OF THE UNIVERSE

I couldn't be
more happy to
be here today!

Yes, I know I
look crabby!

FACES OF THE UNIVERSE

You know, this is
not my best profile
for a picture!

Looking to the left, this face is one of knowledge and confidence.

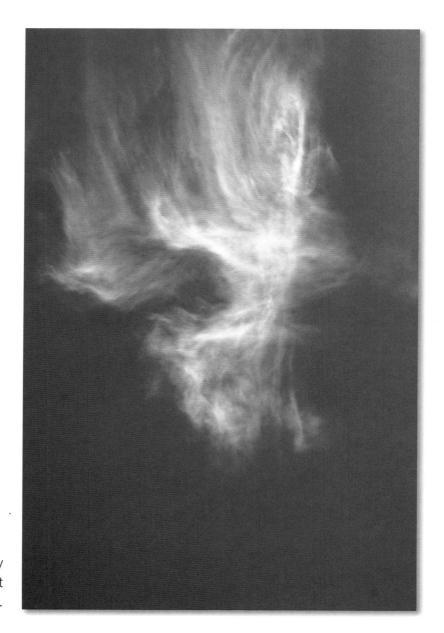

This face and body
are looking to the left
as if juggling balls.

This face is looking to the right. His expression is perhaps one of being above it all.

I can't really believe you said that!

FACES OF THE UNIVERSE

As you can see,
I am very angry!

FACES OF THE UNIVERSE

What? I am stunned
at the news you bring!

This face is looking down to the right. Imagine yourself on a cold winter day in this coat and hood.

FACES OF THE UNIVERSE

I am in
charge
here
now!

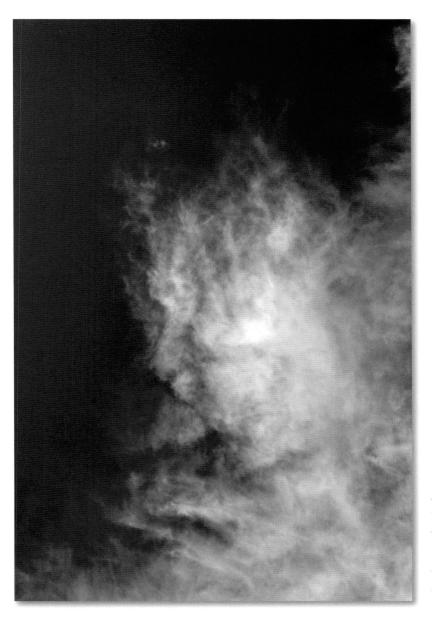

An amazing cloud with two beings with the little one looking directly at you. "I want you to meet my little friend. Isn't he cute?"

Close up of prior
photograph.

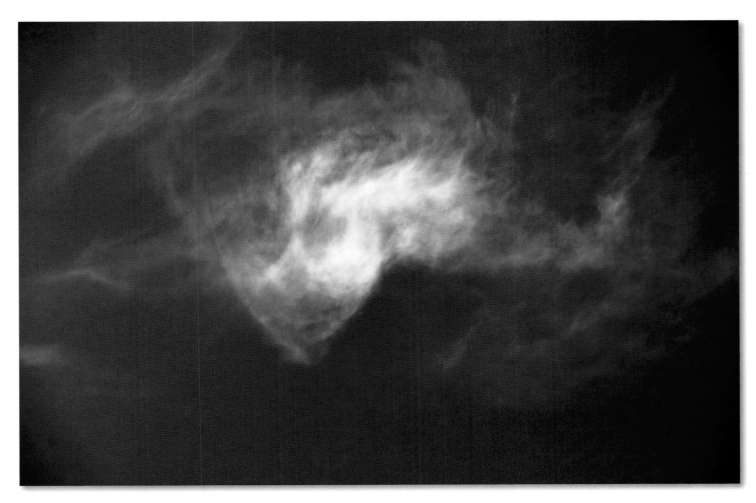

I am always here—watching!

Faces of the Animal Kind

These photographs appear to have faces and forms more like animals we know, or perhaps animals we have never encountered.

Many of them have longer noses or snouts or body forms that remind us of animals.

Gorilla or ape face?

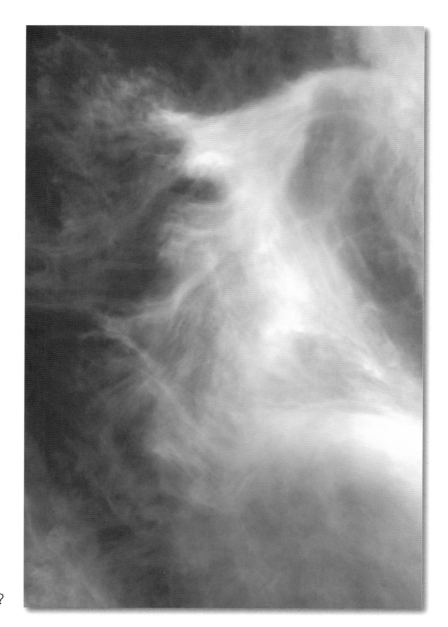

Kangaroo?

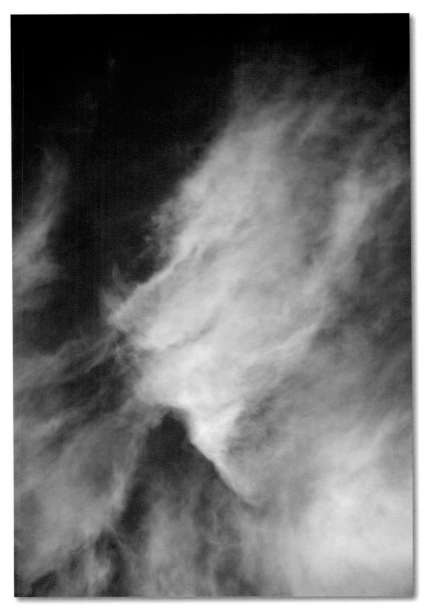

Crazy like a fox?

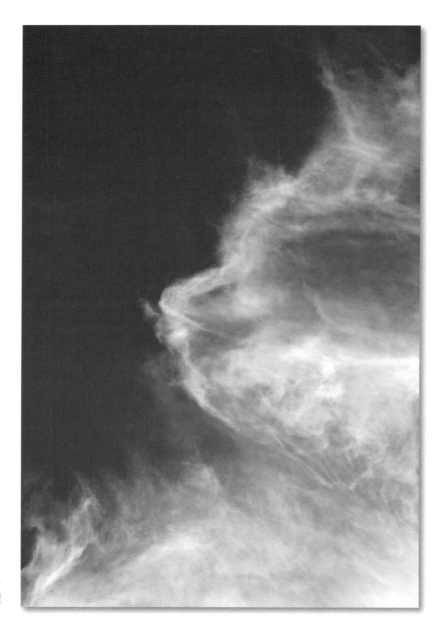

Say that again...
I missed that!

FACES OF THE UNIVERSE

Yes, I do have a
great profile!

I am just
swimming
up-river to
get a bite
to eat!

Just a baby elephant!

FACES OF THE UNIVERSE

A seal should not
have to beg for food!

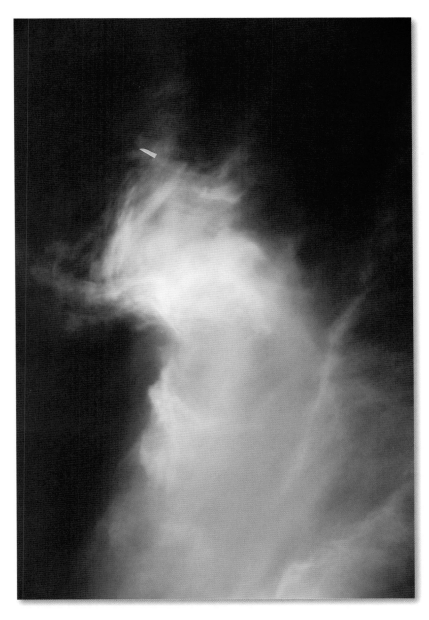

FACES OF THE UNIVERSE

I still say I am not
a rodent!

FACES OF THE UNIVERSE

I have one big eye,
staring right at you!

I am a little mouse, so what!

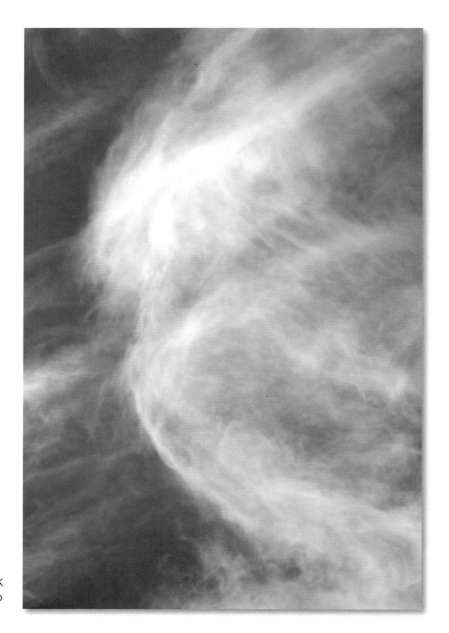

Don't you think
I am cuddly?

Hey, it is nice
to see you
again after all
these years!

No one can
argue I am
a bear!

Hey, look to the right...
even with my long neck,
I can't see what he is
doing?

Look at all those
people down there!
They sure would be
scared if I went down
there to greet them!

I am the cutest lady
here tonight!

Finally! Got this tasty little bug with my tongue!

They all think that a raptor dinosaur can't run fast! I will show them!

Don't I look very
powerful and
in-charge today?

Faces of the Alien Kind

These photographs remind us of faces that we probably care not to see in real life. They just are so different from our comprehension of life and what we are accustomed to on Earth.

What if there are beings like these shown in this chapter? How would we react if we saw them, if we encountered them?

There is such a variety of faces and bodies shown here. Yes, how could these be dreamed up by our clouds? Is there a blueprint somewhere for these images? What if these types of creatures all really existed somewhere in the Universe? And what if they were more intelligent than us human beings?

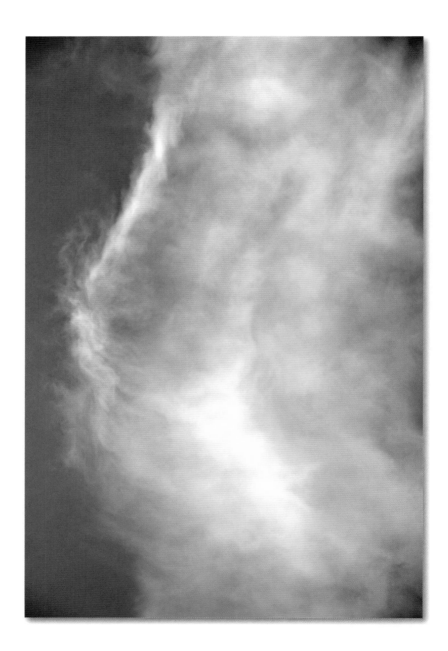

FACES OF THE UNIVERSE

FACES OF THE UNIVERSE

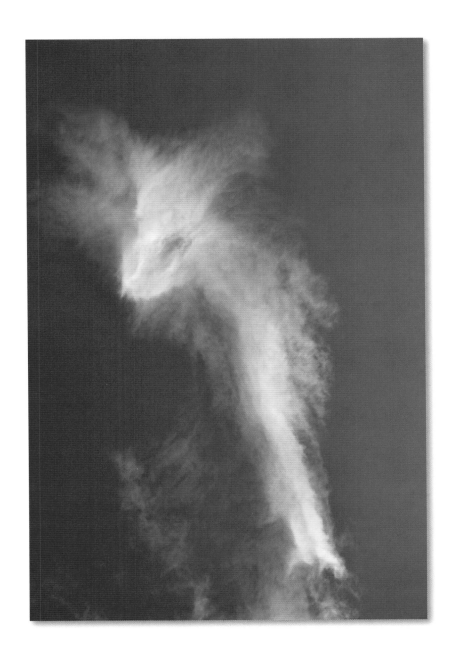

FACES OF THE UNIVERSE

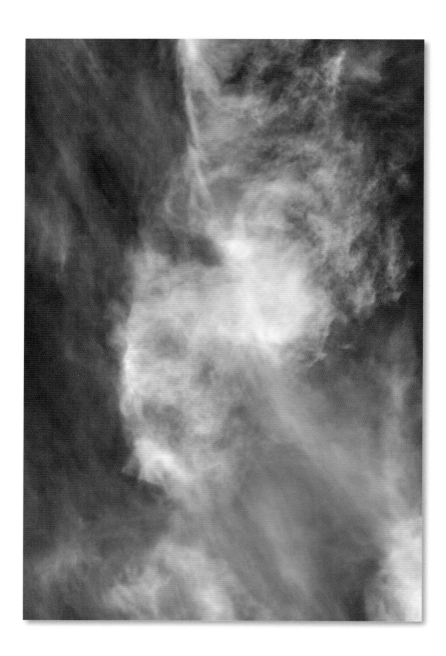

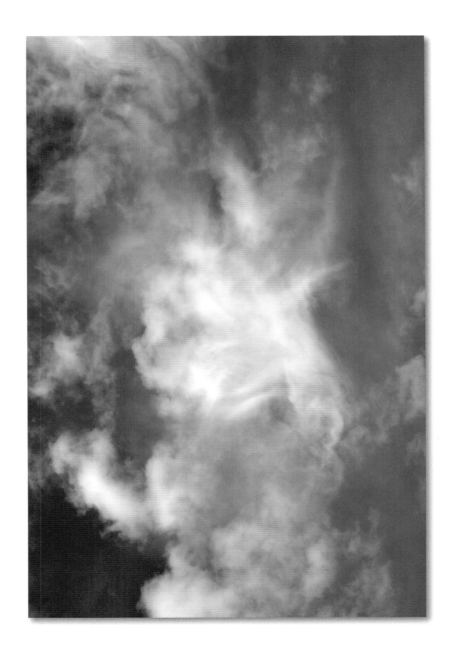

FACES OF THE UNIVERSE

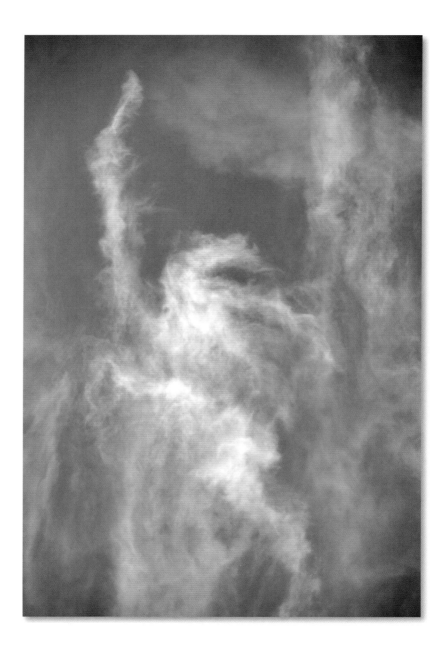

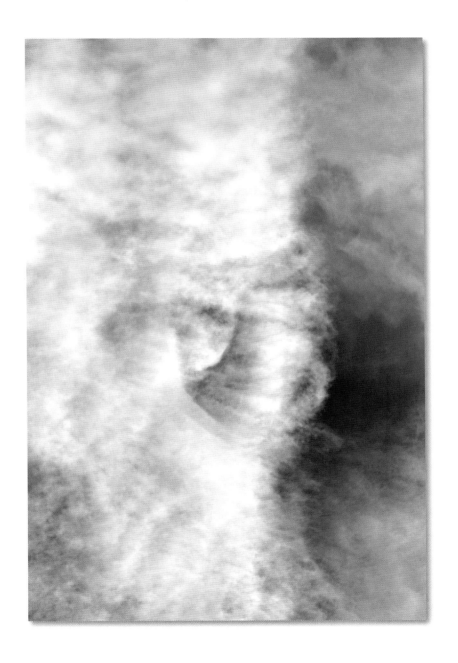

FACES OF THE UNIVERSE

FACES OF THE UNIVERSE

FACES OF THE UNIVERSE

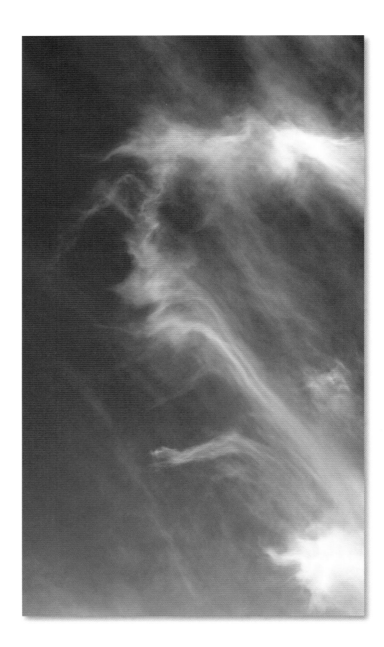

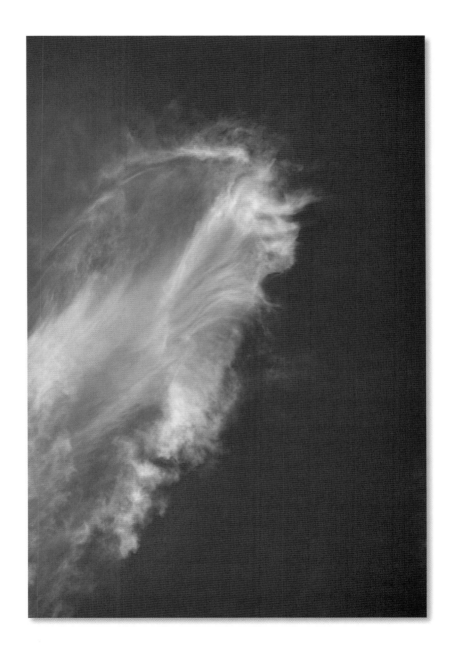

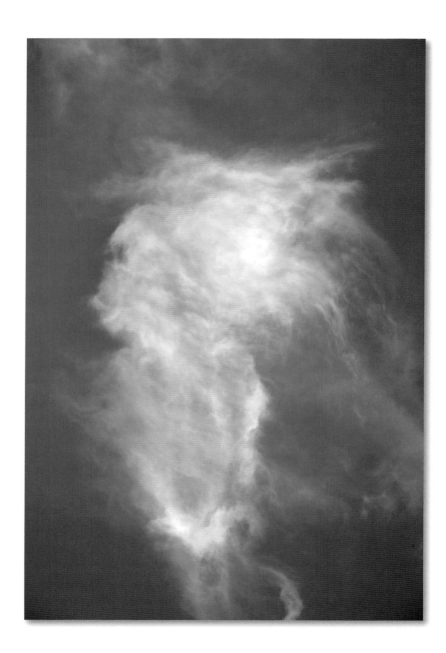

FACES OF THE UNIVERSE

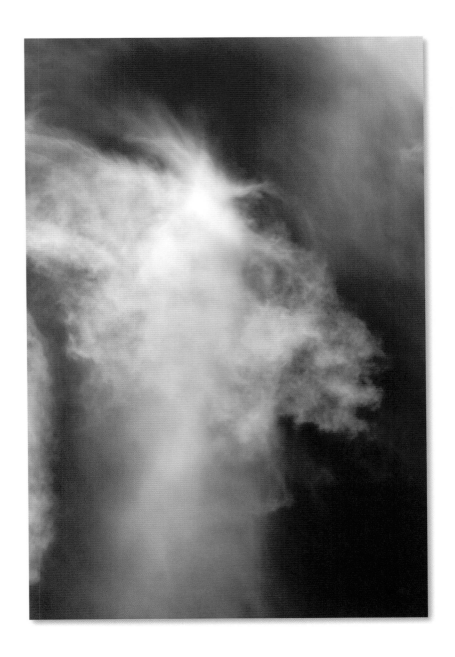

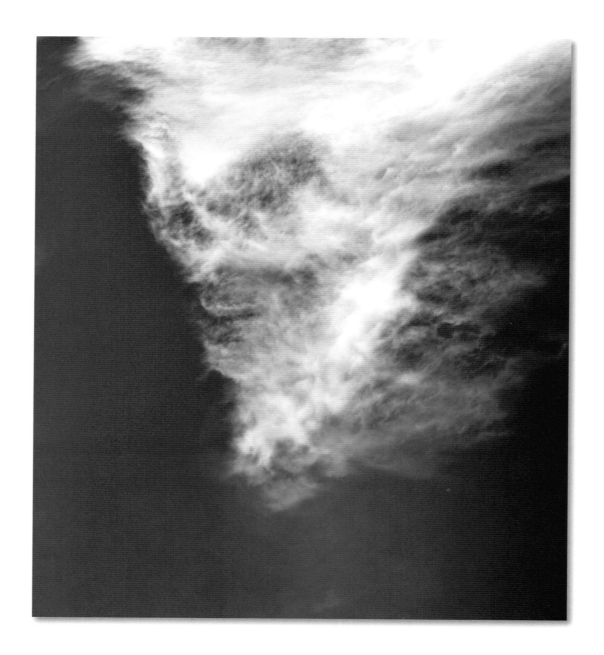

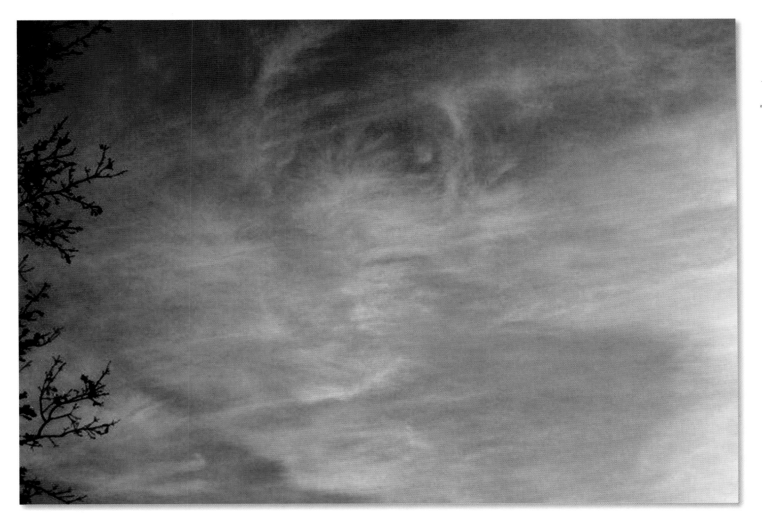

Faces of the Native American Kind

These two photographs perhaps give the impression of having a Native American background. Particularly, the one on page 180 was taken when we were travelling through Navajo Indian lands in northern Arizona.

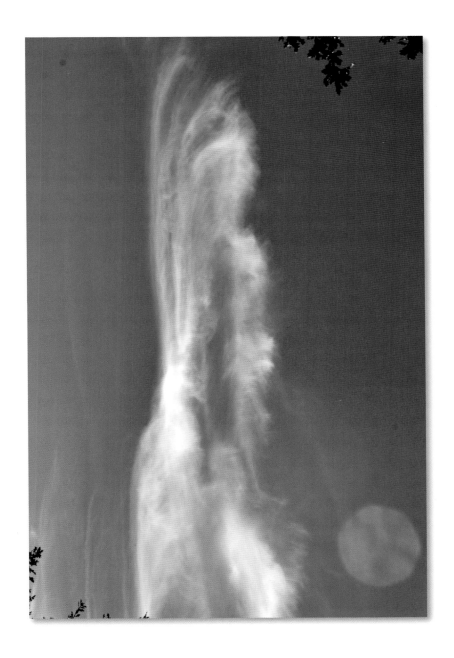

Native
American
face with
headdress
feathers.

Faces of the Cat Kind

These first three photographs were taken while travelling in Arizona near the Sedona area. The first one is of a cat flying through the air, the second of a lion face looking to the right, and the last one is of a cat face looking upward.

The last two were taken in Northern California and appear to be an outline of a common cat head in the sky. You can easily see the head shape, pointed ears, and face pointed to the left.

For us, seeing a cat in the clouds is reassuring. We have had cats in our lives since we first met. Cats are very magical creatures to us and we realize what special animals they are. They are companions, guardians, and partners in our lives.

FACES OF THE UNIVERSE

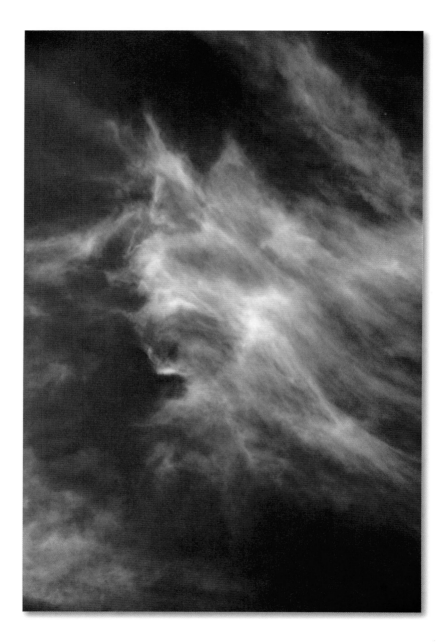

Faces of the Insect Kind

These two photographs have images resembling insects. The first one looks like a spider with the long legs, but in the center it clearly has a face that is very human looking, with two eyes and a mouth with a little smile. The second one reminds us of an ant head and face, with eyes looking right at us and pinchers.

CHAPTER 14

The Merkaba Arrives

This series of photographs, as you will see, is one of the strangest that you might ever encounter. In mid-August 2009, we were leaving a local hospital and went into the parking lot. The sky was very blue that day, peppered with a few white clouds. The clouds, at second glance, were very different for some reason. All of a sudden they seemed to change into incredible forms.

After looking at the pictures we had taken that day, we noticed how different the clouds were. We emailed them quickly to our psychic friend Francie Marie. She replied that they were representing the "gift of the Merkaba," and the "Merkaba" itself.

So we were stunned. We did not know what a Merkaba was!

After researching the Merkaba, we found out. Simply incredible!

According to our research, it appears that the Merkaba is a "vehicle" to travel between dimensions. These earliest definitions come from Ezekiel in the Old Testament of the Bible. Ezekiel apparently defined the Merkaba as the throne chariot of God and described it as a four-wheeled vehicle driven by four cherubim (representing a man, lion, ox, and eagle) each of which has four wings and four faces and which can go in any direction: east, west, north, and south.

Well, we had so many questions. Did we really see the Merkaba? Why did we get to see this Merkaba? Are these definitions of the Merkaba correct? Do you think that there are multiple dimensions? And many more.

What we saw, we are sharing with you on these pages. You be the judge.

The Gift of the Merkaba

In this first series of photographs, the "gift of the Merkaba" is presented. What is shown appears to be a female-looking being. She does not look human, but certainly has a face, eye, nose, and mouth. She has her hand out, facing to the left. In her hand, she has a triangular shaped item. This item is possibly the Merkaba.

In the last photograph, you can now see the entire scene. The female figure to the right is accompanied by a bigger male figure at the left of the photograph. It appears she is gifting this item (The Merkaba) to him.

The Faces of the Merkaba

With this series of photographs, you will see various shots of the creature (the Merkaba) that appeared.

We have to say that to see this incredible cloud creature in the sky above us was breathtaking. How could a cloud look like this? What forces were coming together to make a cloud that appeared to have arms, legs, wings, and a face in the center of it with huge eyes and an unbelievable smile? Can you believe a cloud with a huge smile? What was the meaning of all this that we were experiencing?

We are so glad that we were there, with an available camera to capture these images for this book. We are sure no one would believe us if we just described in words what we saw. A picture, in this case, is worth more than a 1,000 words.

THE FACES OF THE MERKABA

THE FACES OF THE MERKABA

THE FACES OF THE MERKABA

Protector of the Merkaba

This animal-looking cloud was adjacent to the Merkaba cloud, described in the previous sections of this chapter. There was a reason both were in the sky at the same time as this cloud image is the Protector of the Merkaba.

There are two ways to interpret this animal cloud. If you focus on the white image, it appears to be an elephant facing to the right, with one big eye, a small trunk, large body, four legs and small tail.

Alternatively, if you expand your vision and look at the creature's head you can see an outline of the face in a different way. By doing this you see the white face as the left half of the face, and the right half is more in an outline of white and blue. Now you can see a whole face with two eyes, nose, mouth, and one ear.

The creature appears to be another kind of animal...an animal that is very strong like a Wolf. To us, it appears to be protecting its companion, the Merkaba.

The third photograph shows the Protector as it is breaking up in the sky as the cloud is changing over time. Even as it breaks up, it appears to be three creatures in a row with the creature at the right with a face and smile.

What does this all mean? The clouds of the Merkaba and the Protector where so remarkable that they had to be the front and back covers of this book. As such, they are together again in this book as they were in the sky that day.

PROTECTOR OF THE MERKABA

PROTECTOR OF THE MERKABA

CHAPTER 15

Faces of the Angels

After many experiences in our lives, we have come to believe that angels are with each of us on planet Earth.

Perhaps these clouds in these two photographs can provide some evidence.

In the first photograph, there is a beautiful cloud that seems to have life, showing its wings spread like an angel.

More incredibly, the second photograph was taken in Sedona, Arizona in 2008 while we were walking a labyrinth. At the conclusion of the walk/ meditation, this cloud formed directly over our heads. We were speechless and immediately took this picture.

In looking at this photograph, we think you can readily see an angel, which we think is Archangel Michael, as he is often depicted in historical literature on a horse. In this cloud formation, he is on a horse as you can see its eye, head, and Michael's leg coming down at the left side of the photograph, as if he is on a saddle.

We were so privileged to see this and experience it. We are still in awe every time we see this photograph. You, as the reader, might have another explanation for this image. Why did this cloud form? What is its message?

But one thing for sure is that seeing is believing! Our camera captured something very special that day!

FACES OF THE ANGELS

FACES OF THE EARTH

This image was imbedded in a sidewalk. It appears to depict the image of a Native American in full ceremonial dress, or it has some similarities to a Mayan, Aztec, or Inca peoples.

CHAPTER 17

Faces of the Earth

We have asked you to look up, taken you to the skies and the wonder and life of the clouds. Now we ask you to look down, to the wonder that is in the Earth. Who would think that the unique images that are presented to you in this chapter would be in rocks, stones, and concrete sidewalks?

These images raise a lot of questions. How could such images be inside rocks and sidewalks? Who did it? What is being communicated? What is the purpose?

One explanation might be "Elementals." Some believe that elementals are mythical creatures in the air, water, fire, and earth. Some say that Elementals are such things as elves, fairies, gnomes, etc. Perhaps such beings have the ability to manifest in stones and sidewalks as shown in the next series of photographs.

This image is in a large rock showing what appears to be a father figure at the left talking to his son at the right.

This and the next photograph appear to show again images of Native Americans talking to each other, perhaps a parent and child.

Close-up of
previous photo.

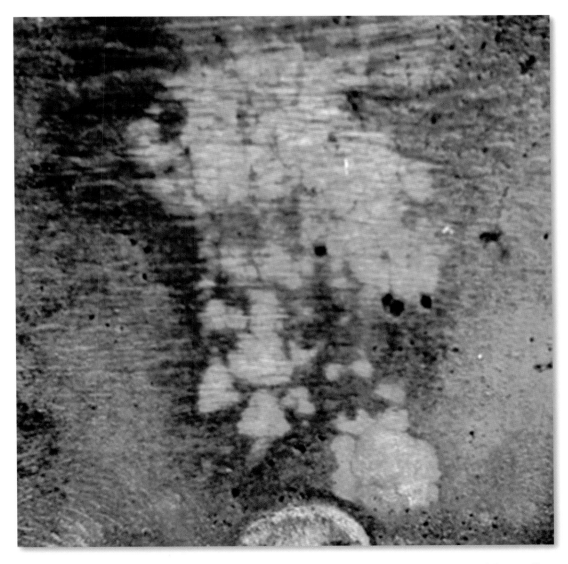

This image looks like a Native American chief, looking to the left. This is a side profile of a face, with nose, eye, and headdress.

This rock is very unique. It is five-sided first of all and was found in Flagstaff, Arizona. Each side has an image in black. Each image appears to reflect an appearance of a Native American.

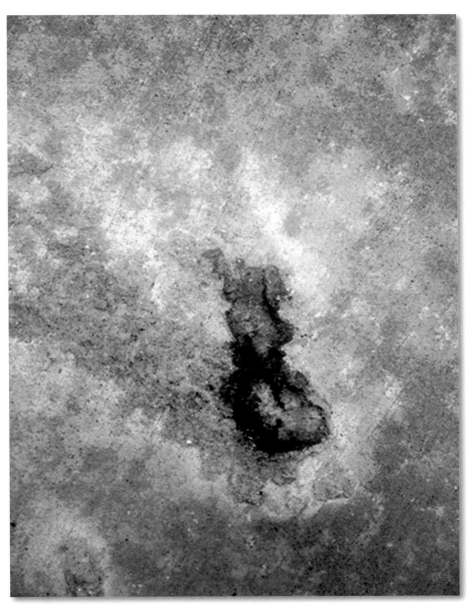

This image is in a sidewalk. It is simply extraordinary. It appears to show an elephant-shaped creature looking up, with its trunk up in the air. One can make out the eyes, the trunk, large ears, and body.

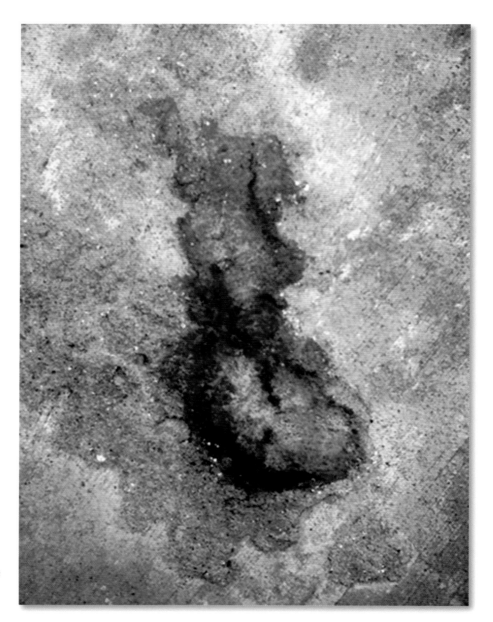

Close-up of
previous photo.

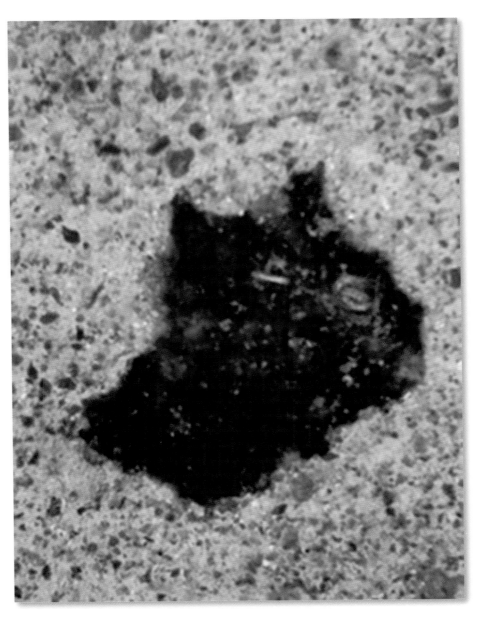

This image is of a black cat in a sidewalk, facing to the right. One can see the ears, eye, snout, and mouth.

This image in a sidewalk is what appears to be an animal such as a wolf, dog, or coyote on top of its kill. It is facing to the left, with head pointing upward.

This image
in a sidewalk
appears to be
an animal like
a dog standing
on something.

This image in a sidewalk shows a little cat or kitten. One can make out the ears, eyes, nose and mouth, and perhaps even the whiskers.

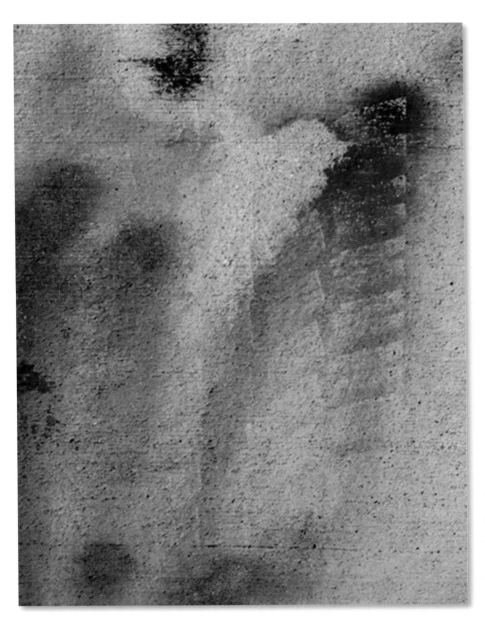

This image in a sidewalk perhaps shows a family of birds. They may even be penguin-like in form.

This rock face appears to resemble a turtle. It was found in Hawaii along the coast where turtles assemble.

This rock appears to have a face of a beagle dog pointing to the right. One can see the dog ears, nose, and eye in the darker color.

This image in a rock shows a large head facing to the left. It shows two large eye sockets, a mouth, and large forehead. The skull or head is in the center in the darker color with the brown color forming the outline of the head.

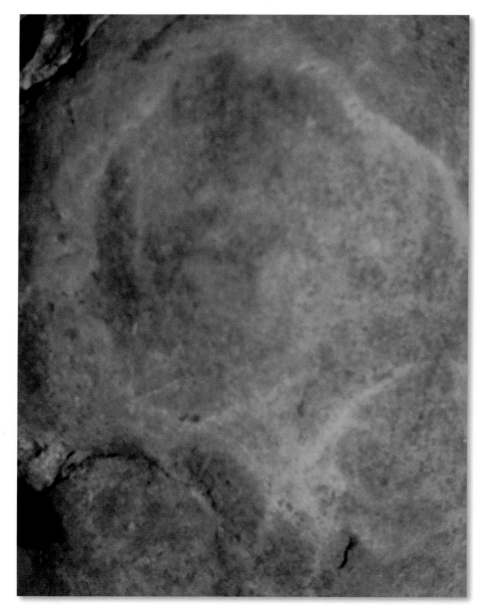

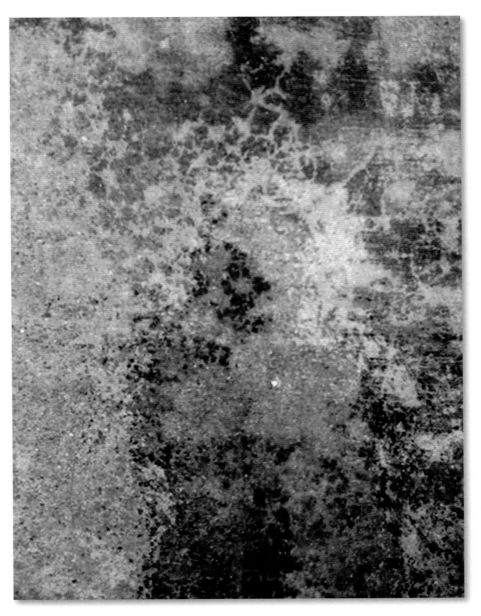

This image in a sidewalk shows a face pointing left, with eyes and mouth.

This image is a large rock formation just off the coast of Hawaii. One can see the face and openings for two eyes, and a large open mouth.

This sidewalk image shows in the white color, forms of a human-type man figure looking left and embracing a smaller figure, perhaps an animal.

FACES OF THE EARTH

This image in a road shows a procession of beings in black, ascending upwards to the right.

This sidewalk image shows two human figures with their backs to us. They appear to be women with hats and long robes. They are shown by the lighter color outline. Also, at the bottom right of the photograph is a lion lying at the feet of the two women, and the lion is facing to the right with its mouth wide open. One can see the lion's mouth and eyes formed by the black color.

This is a black piece of tar! These two images are a piece of tar material laying flat on the concrete gutter. Looking closely, one can make out a face pointing to the left. The face has an eye, nose, and one small ear is showing. Below the face is a lighter color in a heart shape, where a heart might be.

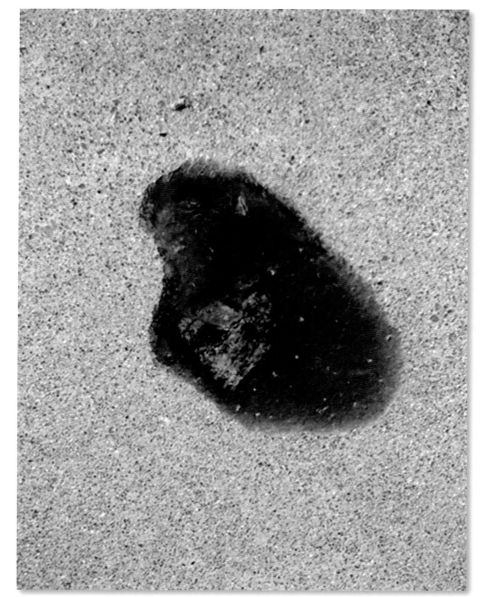

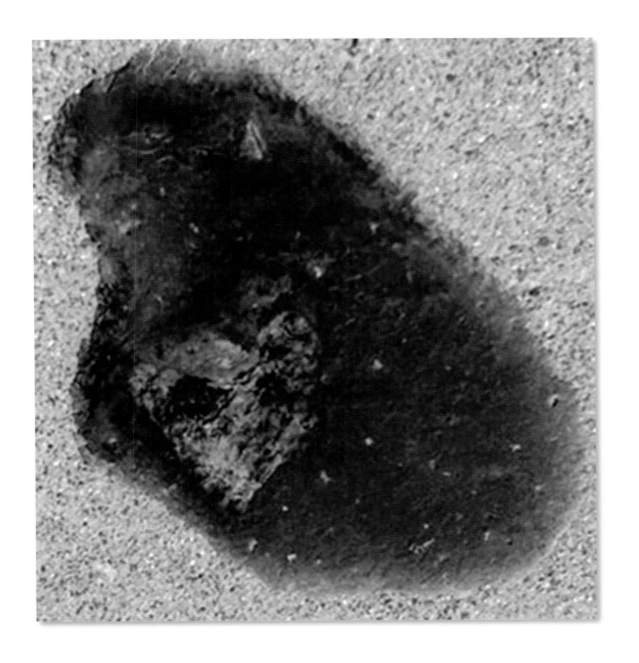

This image in a sidewalk appears to be a face pointing left. The profile of the face is the darker material. This face appears to reflect an appearance like one would see of ancient Roman figures or rulers. The face has discernable curly hair, large nose, and large lips.

This image in a sidewalk appears to show two beings standing and attached back-to-back. One image faces left, the other right so we are seeing profiles of each. The left image appears to be an animal like a bull, with a bull-type face, horns, and even a hoof. The other being is human in appearance with a nose and mouth.

In a sidewalk,
this image is of
royal ceremonial
staffs similar to
those depicted in
ancient cultures

The next three images of the same rock show an image in the center. This image appears to be of a woman, as if sitting on a floor and her body pointing to the right. She has a child in her lap, but the child is standing and its arm is shown around the woman's head or neck area. The woman's arm is shown holding the child at its feet.

The next two sidewalk images shown in the darker color depict several beings. There are such images at the upper right, center, and right of center.

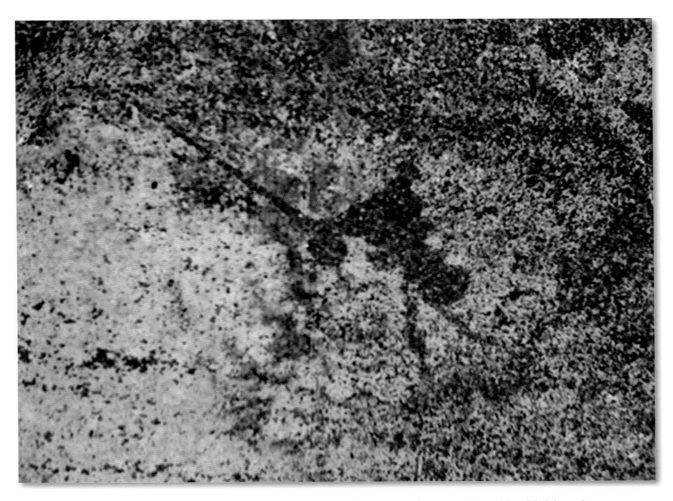

The center image has been enlarged and appears to be an ancient soldier with shield and spear, head, body, and two legs.

These two images are of a green rock we got as a gift from our friend Kathleen. The first rock image is at the time we received the gift. The second image is now. One can see the rock has changed color. In addition, there are two images of beings inside the face of the rock, one of which has the face of a cat-like creature.

CHAPTER 18

Faces of the Paranormal Kind

This chapter is about paranormal and alien events. These are mostly images that you need a camera to capture, as we cannot see them with just our eyes.

In our opinion, these images suggest that there are multiple dimensions, portals, elemental creatures, and alien presence. Each photograph has its own story that we hope you will enjoy.

The photograph to the left was given to us by our friend Kathleen Scott, and she has donated it for use in this book. It was taken in the foothills of northern California, in a rural area. One can see the lighted area which appears to be a portal with a being coming through the opening. If you look at the perimeter of the lighter area in the center, you can see a rigid rectangular opening, shaped similar to a window. Inside this "window" a lighted being is coming through.

In the center of this photograph is a Buddha concrete statue. This Buddha was given to us by Kathleen Scott as she could not keep it any longer. She says it was blessed by the Tibetan Monks. We put it in our backyard. Our psychic friend Francie Marie suggested that we take pictures of it at night as she was feeling something special would occur. It certainly did. This one photograph shows a wispy light coming straight up from the Buddha for about 10 feet, then changing into a ball of bright light, and then that bright light goes off into the sky to the left. This was all done in the split second of the camera shutter.

We are on the Big Island of Hawaii at the top of the mountain, Mauna Kea, where the many large telescopes and observatories are located. At this 14,000 foot elevation, nothing is living and the ground is all gravel and rock.

We are looking down from the top of the mountain and west to see the sunset. We put a large crystal down the mountain side as you can see by the white shaft like material at the lower left. There is nothing near that crystal in the first photograph. In the second photograph, there are two little orange-yellow beings at or on top of the crystal. You can faintly see these transparent beings as they have eyes and a mouth.

What is the explanation for these creatures? Hawaiian legend has it that there are elemental beings called Minihunnas that live on the islands. Perhaps this is what we captured with our camera.

The next two photographs were taken in Egypt in 2008, at the Ramesses statue in the Temple of Luxor.

There are three rather alien things seen in these pictures. First is the circular white globes, often called Orbs. There is much speculation about what these are...spirits, angels, or other entities.

Second, notice the light orange head-like feature on top of the shoulder of the statue. This head appears to be alien in form, with eyes, mouth, and interesting diagonal lines on its face at the cheek area.

Third, notice the black outlined image on the orange colored wall behind the statue. This image is alien in appearance with a large head, large eyes, long body, and maybe hoof like feet.

FACES OF THE PARANORMAL KIND

The next five photographs tell the story of possible alien or extraterrestrial visitations to our planet. The photographs were taken in Sedona, Arizona, but the story is about Sedona and South Africa.

In a 2008 visit to Sedona, we took a tour with our guide "Storm" to visit sacred and spiritual sites and especially areas with petroglyphs. We asked to see any petroglyphs that showed flying saucers, so Storm took us to an area south of Sedona in the mountains. After climbing to a rather remote area on a mountainside cliff, we found a large variety of petroglyphs. We found one, as seen in this photograph, that was shaped like a flying saucer. It had an oval shape, four legs shaped like poles, and a landing area feature at its side like a ladder or entry. We felt sure we had an image of a flying saucer, which could have been carved in that cliff for thousands of years.

In another photograph, one can see the image of a saber-toothed tiger, which apparently has been extinct for up to 10,000 years. This also shows strange looking creatures at the bottom of the image with long legs. Could it be that the saber-toothed tiger image in this photograph could date the flying saucer to thousands of years ago as the saber-toothed tiger became extinct perhaps 10,000 years ago?

With the next photographs came some confirmation. On the following day, after seeing the flying saucer image in the cliff, we went out for breakfast in Sedona. The restaurant was closed at 9 a.m. but we scouted around in the same building and found a storefront called The Ringing Rocks Foundation. This was a place to honor and preserve the shamans and healers from around the world. In this place, were artifacts of each shaman's culture, pictures of each shaman, and books that each shaman had written.

As we were carefully looking at each exhibit, which were presented in a similar fashion to that seen in a museum, we found the exhibit of Vusamazulu Credo Mutwa, the shaman from South Africa. The exhibit had photographs of him, and parts of his culture.

What caught our attention was the large necklace he wore, a Blood Necklace. It was no coincidence that we got to visit The Ringing Rocks Foundation and this shaman from South Africa. In one of the photographs of a close up of the necklace he is wearing, you can see in the lower part of the necklace, left of center, the shape and configuration of the identical flying saucer we happened to find in the Sedona petroglyphs the day before. On his necklace, you can see the oval shape of the saucer, the same four legs in the same location, and the ladder or entry is there but in a different location of the saucer. A close up is seen in the last photograph.

So there you have it. The flying saucer shaped image in Sedona's mountains, perhaps thousands of years old, is now found on the necklace of the South African shaman, half a world away. Perhaps this information on his necklace was passed down to him from his ancestors.

Vusamazulu Credo Mutwa does explain that he did visit parts of Africa and that he found a tribe of strange beings called Bantwana (Children of the Stars). He said that they were very human looking except that they had hooves for feet and legend has it that they came from the star Sirius long ago.

We invite you to visit The Ringing Rocks Foundation in Sedona. We also want to specially thank The Ringing Rocks Foundation for giving us permission in December 2009 to use these photographs taken inside their facility. A special thanks to Steve Denorscia for working with us on this request to use the photographs. You may reach the Foundation through the Internet or by phone at (928) 282-1298.

FACES OF THE PARANORMAL KIND

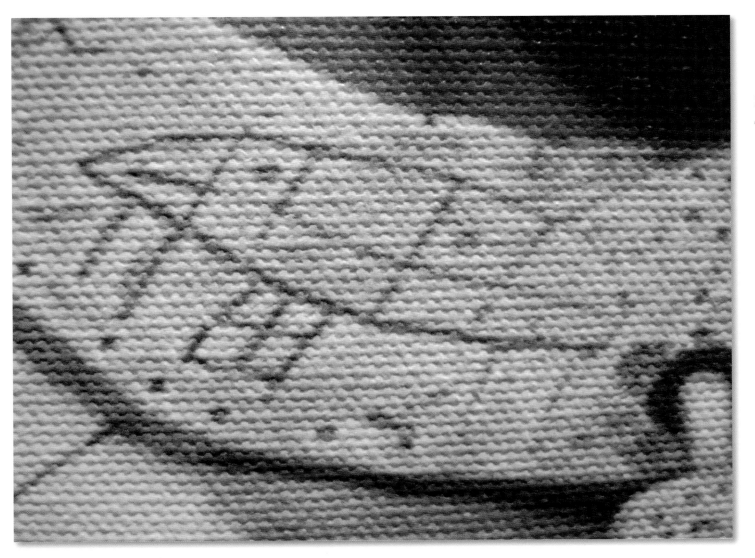

Sand worm from the beach at St. Malo, France

CHAPTER 19

The Passion, the Love, and the Magic

We hope you have enjoyed *Faces of the Universe*. It has taken us years to assemble this book through thousands of photographs and extensive travel.

This book is an expression of our Passion to find answers about the world around us, to think the unthinkable, to see the unseen, to imagine the impossible.

We have tried to create a comprehensive visual presentation of images of our world not often talked about or explored. Passion for the world around us, the earth, and each other continue to amaze and inspire us to continue on this journey.

We bring this information to you with our Love. Love for all things on this planet.

Expressions of Love can come in many forms...

THE PASSION, THE LOVE, AND THE MAGIC

...perhaps like the photograph of the dogs on the beach in France...

...or the llamas at Machu Picchu, in Peru.

One of our expressions of Love for each other has been a renewal of our vows and commitment to each other at sacred locations around the world. It started at Machu Picchu, Peru, very spontaneously, and we have continued this practice at many other locations that feel special to us, such as Stonehenge, the top of Mauna Kea Hawaii, and at the Kom Ombo Temple on the Nile in Egypt.

During each of our special trips, we try to find rings for each other. While looking for rings in Egypt, we found two gold rings that were similar, the only two in a tiny shop. However, the rings were very small and seemed to only fit our little fingers. We purchased them anyway because they were uniquely inscribed with Egyptian symbols and seemed perfect for our ceremony.

That evening in the Temple, we decided to try them on our ring fingers, and magically, they both fit. It was clearly meant that we wear them as a symbol of our love and commitment, and they have remained on those fingers since that evening.

Then there is the Magic—the Magic of all things on this planet and in our universe. The Raven represents this magic to us.

The ravens have guided us in many of our adventures. The first time we encountered their energy and magic was in Sedona, Arizona. Ravens were always with us in England and eleven ravens came to us in a pouring rainstorm as we were leaving Stonehenge and seemed to "speak" to us. They often lead us when we are lost. They are our guides.

A special raven, depicted in this photograph, was waiting for us at the rim of the Grand Canyon. They have always been magical in myth and legend and we continue to feel their energy and presence.

As the raven represents the Magic of life, we believe we should honor the Magic of life and the opportunities it brings.

In our journeys, we must have the freedom to explore without limitations of space, time, or convention. What better way to find our answers to life than to fly and see like the bird.

With sincere Passion, Love, and Magic,

Tom and Carol Lumberg

YOU MAY CONTACT US AT OUR WEBSITE:
WHENANGELSTOUCH.COM
EMAIL: TOM@WHENANGELSTOUCH.COM